G000097733

To My Child: Things to Remember

Forever & Always

To My Child:
Things to Remember

Forever & Always

Written By: Jeannie Honey Culbertson-Crow

Preface

Recently, in 2020, three key things happened in my life (among the many life-challenges we all faced as a general populace in 2020). I lost my job and became a work-from-home mom, one of my friends passed away from cancer (leaving her three young children behind), and my oldest son (age 19) prepared to leave the nest to begin a life of his own, amongst the chaos we now know as 2020.

From the ashes of my life, I began building my own business from the ground up. I was devastated when my friend Wendy passed away. It hit me extremely hard, mostly because I was faced with my own legacy. What would I tell my own children today, if knew with certainty I wouldn't be here tomorrow? After all, none of us are guaranteed a tomorrow, are we?

Of my six children, my oldest son has always had the strongest of wills (his name literally translated means "spear, battle, or little warrior") and we often have a battle of wills (where do you think he gets it from?). He has a protective nature and good intentions, even if he has a hard head. More often than not, at the end of the day, I still have to reassure him how special he is to me and how much I love him—and when you put it all together, that's where the idea for this book was born. It is a collection of truths I have told him over the years, as well as age-old advice passed down from generations.

I made this book at home on a laptop, printed it, and sent it with him when he moved out, so that he would always have a reminder that he will always be my little boy (even though he's taller than me and outweighs me by about 40 pounds), whether I'm 37 years old as I am now, 97 years old, or up in heaven watching over him, hopefully someday in the long and distant future. I also wanted other parents to have the same opportunity to pass this special gift on to their own children, too.

Jeannie Honey Culbertson-Crow ~ The Noteworthy Mom

Introduction

Ellen Cantarow once said, "Making the decision to have a child—it's momentous. It is to decide forever to have your heart go walking around outside your body." And, boy, is it ever. You know if your phone or wallet were to grow legs and begin walking around, you'd want to keep that precious thing very close to you. But as your baby grows, and ventures further and further away, your heartstrings pull harder— it's painful and scary, those moments, as your child grows up and ventures out into the world.

As a mother, it starts at birth, the very moment they leave your womb. The doctor takes your baby away, to check for breathing, clear the airway, cut the cord. Sometimes, my babies were taken across the room to be cared for. Some babies are in trouble, needing surgery or extra care. Then, grandma, grandpa, aunts, and uncles want to hold little precious. *Please don't leave the room with my baby,* especially if it's a firstborn!

It continues. First day of daycare. First day of pre-school, kindergarten. The first sleepover. Those moments when your precious heart gets out of sight. Then, high school comes, and you're lucky if they still speak to you. Hugs are less frequent. They're driving now. That's a tough one. Girlfriends, boyfriends, high school dances. Their first job. When was the last time you saw them?

Then... High school graduation. College, maybe. The day comes when it's time to move out. The final moment when your precious heart is leaving for the long-term. This moment, which all the little moments and stretches of time have been preparing you for, getting longer and harder in between, is finally here.

When you cannot be there every day to remind them to be good, be safe, take care of themselves and how much you love them, don't worry—they know. But this book is a great way to remind them. Your heart is now out there, every single day. As a parent, it can be difficult. I think this book is one way to help cope with that, easing the transition, for both parents and their adult children.

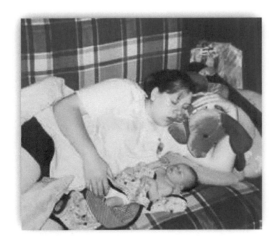

Our First Day

You entered this world half-asleep and innocent,

Choosing your perfect moment.

You saved my life that day,

Though you probably didn't know it.

You chose me, and chose you,

The day you made me a mom.

Call Me, Any Time

Part of being a mom is letting you fall,

Letting you fail, letting you learn.

That does not mean I do not watch,

Or I do not care for you, my darling.

I am here to catch you and I always will be,

No matter how old you are—anytime, anywhere, so call me.

A Mother's Prayer

A mother's prayers are all she has after her baby bird has left the nest.

Your mom will pray for you because she can't protect you everywhere you go.

Don't forget about your mom. Call her occasionally and keep in touch.

She's going to give you space so you can figure out who you really are without her.

If she's done her job well, you have turned out alright and she knows this.

She's going to give you that space to do what you need to do.

But she loves you, misses you, and prays for you daily.

Live Simply

Always put aside money for the week and never live beyond your means.

Cheap cars drive from point A to B the same as expensive ones.

Do your best to cash-flow your life and don't rely on loans or credit cards.

Remember: debt-free and financial freedom both indicate freedom in your life.

Debts multiply and create hardship and burdens that are difficult to get out of.

Don't borrow money you can't repay. Save money often, pay yourself first.

If you want to keep your friends, don't borrow money from them.

A Little Respect Goes a Long Way

If you don't have the money to pay your bills, your debt collector will be much more

understanding if you call and explain than if you just don't call them.

Most of the time you can set up a payment plan.

The same goes if you're running late for an appointment.

Always call and explain.

If you don't, they may not allow you to come back.

A little respect goes a long way.

Give to Charity

What goes around comes around, so whatever you put out there comes back.

If you want good to come to you, remember to do random acts of kindness.

Forgive often, and love like you haven't been hurt.

Forgive yourself for your mistakes, it's how you grow.

You've watched other's lives go down in flames, and you've watched others become successful.

Follow the examples of success. Learn from other's mistakes.

Give to charity and tithe. Give without expecting anything in return.

Never Question Your Worth

Never look outside yourself for validation of your worth.

Someone once told me, "God didn't make junk."

The Bible says, "Before I formed you in the womb, I knew you,

before you were born, I set you apart," (Jerimiah 1:1).

This verse tells us that our souls were created at the beginning of time,

and we knew God in heaven before we were born.

Don't ever let anyone make you feel like you don't matter.

You have all the validation you need just by looking in a mirror.

But, if that's not enough, just know how much your mom loves you by giving you this book.

Go the Extra Mile

When living with other people, don't forget to shower and clean up after yourself daily.

Do your laundry at least once a week.

While it seems like a small task, just because you're an adult and no

one can tell you what to do, a little common courtesy goes a long way.

Go the extra mile once in a while and clean up the kitchen and living area by yourself.

Offer to pay for dinner occasionally.

Just show a little extra care, kindness, and initiative.

It's a lot harder for your roommates to stay mad at you if you do a little extra every now and again.

Buy a Planner, Set a Schedule

Make sure you set a schedule for yourself.

You'll find that once you're out on your own, you feel like you don't have a plan.

It can leave you feeling aimless and empty. You'll contemplate the meaning of life.

Create life goals. Write them down. Put them in your planner. Get excited about them.

Use a calendar, either in your phone, or preferably, buy a physical

planner that you can use to look at daily to make a schedule.

Set a day of the week to do laundry, and a day of the week or month to plan your bills.

Make sure you do your laundry weekly and plan your bills monthly.

You Choose How You Feel

Each day as you go into the world you'll run into all kinds of people.

Some will be kind, others will not. Don't let them ruin your whole day.

Be considerate of others. You don't know what they might be going through.

So, whatever you do today, do it with kindness in your heart.

If someone is unkind to you, you don't have to be unkind to them.

You're bigger and better if you manage to walk away without responding in anger.

Remember: how people treat you says more about them than it does about you.

You decide how you're going to feel, every day. So, create your own happiness!

Set Personal Boundaries

People will often be unkind to you, be kind anyway.

Sometimes your kindness will be the only kindness they will ever see in their world of misery.

That being said, you need to set boundaries and limits.

You must have self-respect by setting boundaries or others will take advantage of you.

A lack of personal boundaries invites a lack of respect.

You can be a good person, with a kind heart, and still say, "no."

Some Good Habits Are Better Than None

You already know to eat right, include healthy foods in your diet, and take care of your teeth.

Even if you don't eat right all the time, try to throw in a few healthy foods each week.

Eat late at night less often as possible and check your weight weekly.

Getting enough sleep is essential to your weight and your health.

Go to the park or join a gym. Don't wait until your weight is out of control.

Even if you forget to floss daily, make sure you set a specific

day of the week to brush really well, floss, and use a good mouthwash.

Go After Your Dreams

Never be afraid to dream and never give up on your dreams.

If you really want something, you'll find a way to make it happen.

Don't have a closedminded mentality, or a smallminded mentality. Dream big!

Even if we come from humble beginnings, it doesn't mean we can't find a way to make it happen.

I hope I have shown you enough of the world during your

childhood for you to see there is more to life than this. Go get it.

Imagine where you want to be when you're my age,

what you want to become, and what you want to do with your life.

Picture it and go for it!

Overcome Your Fears

Sometimes in life you won't want to start.

Your next project. Your next day. Your next relationship.

Whatever that next BIG step may be.

It seems so overwhelming and you don't know where to start, or how.

You can always grab my hand, figuratively, or literally.

I'll walk beside you and help you through it.

I still get scared and overwhelmed sometimes. That's okay.

You just have to push through it. You'll be glad you did.

If you don't, your fear will grow, and become harder to overcome.

Keep Only What Sparks Your Joy

Life is too short to hold grudges, let them go.

Sometimes, random people suck, let them go, too.

And sometimes, your "friends" drain your energy.

You begin to realize you have nothing left to give, because you can't get anything from an empty vessel.

You keep people around longer than they deserve because you're loyal.

Ask yourself if they bring value to your life and if they really value **you**, or just what you do for them.

If they don't truly bring value to your life, let them go, too.

In your life, keep only what sparks your joy.

Ignorance is No Excuse

Never allow a lack of knowledge stop you from your accomplishments.

You can learn anything you choose if you really want to.

The internet has a plethora of information.

Take a class or watch a tutorial. Talk to people and ask questions.

And, as always, you can ask your parents for help.

I want you to go farther in life than I ever dreamed.

I believe in you. You have so much potential!

You have your whole life ahead of you.

You can accomplish anything you set your mind to!

The Snowball Effect

If you've ever rolled a snowball, you know how it grows.

It is the same in life.

When accomplishing goals, or ignoring crises, refer to the snowball effect.

A crisis will grow if you ignore it, so deal with it as soon as possible.

Otherwise, it will get out of hand, fast.

When tackling tasks, do one thing at a time, starting with the smallest one first.

When tackling debts, focus extra income on the smallest one first.

You'll find that you'll accomplish your goals faster this way.

Live Each Day Like It's Your Last

All parents usually know the first time their baby said mama or dada.

Or when their baby took their first steps.

But we never know the "lasts." The last kiss. The last time you slept in our bed.

The last time we picked you up and carried you around on our hip.

Live responsibly, as in, don't spend your last dime, but live each day as if it may be your last.

One day, you'll give your last hug, kiss your last kiss goodbye.

You'll hear someone's voice the last time, but you'll never know when it will be the last time.

Live every day as if it were the last time you will be with the person you love.

Never Stop Learning

Keeping your mind active is as important as keeping your body active.

Learning is exercise for your brain, and the human mind craves knowledge.

Depriving your brain of knowledge is called learning starvation.

This has negative effects on your health—a very good reason to never stop learning.

If you don't use your brain in new and different ways,

you lose connections within your brain, making it harder to learn, later.

The more you learn, the better you get at learning.

There is always something new to learn!

Don't Be Afraid to Make Mistakes

"If you're not making mistakes, then you're not doing anything."

~ John Wooden

You're going to make mistakes, don't be afraid of them. Learn from them.

Own up to your mistakes or you'll never grow.

If you need help or guidance, don't be afraid to talk to your parents.

Much like when you were little and your mom kissed your boo-boos, when you're sad

your mom will still try to make it better, even if you messed up.

Always remember, put more good into this world than you take from it.

Your mom is **always** proud of you, no matter what.

And I love you, forever and always!

Acknowledgments

I would like to thank my husband Cody, first and foremost, for his patience with me as I navigate the ever-changing waters of Noteworthy Mom. What began in a pandemic being let go from my job, and becoming a full-time stay-at-home mom, has become a full-time exploration of who I can become and how far I can go as a wife, mother, entrepreneur, blogger, and free-spirited, goal-driven Capricorn. He has been my rock and his never-ending support has kept me going.

I want to thank my children, because without them I wouldn't be here today. And, I want to thank their father, Jerry, for without him, they wouldn't be here.

I would also like to thank my son Kane, for whom this book was written. Thank you for inspiring me, for being my friend, and for saving my life.

Thank you all for your love and support through all these years. I love each and every one of you; you all know this, but it never hurts to say it just one more time!

I also want to give credit to the amazing artists on Pixabay, for the free-to-use photos I was granted permission to use in this book. I especially want to give credit to Beate Bachmann, the artist of the beautiful baby photo that is my cover photo. Without Pixabay and the artists who make these stock photos available, my book wouldn't have been possible.

And, finally, to my readers, thank you! Thank you for purchasing my book. It means so much to me.